A BUTTERFLY AFRAID TO FLY

A Butterfly Afraid to Fly

AN INSPIRATIONAL BOOK OF POEMS

SUMMER HEAT

A DIVINE JOURNEY
Atlanta, Georgia

A DIVINE JOURNEY
An imprint of Grace Royal International, LLC
Atlanta, GA
www.graceroyal-intl.com

Copyright © 2021 by Summer Heat
Cover Art: Felton J. "Bud" Galliano

All rights reserved. No part of this book may be reproduced by a mechanical, photographic, or electronic process; nor may any parts of this book be stored in any retrieval system without the written permission of the publisher.

Published in the United States of America by A Divine Journey, an imprint of Grace Royal International LLC, Atlanta, GA. For additional information, including bulk shipping options, address Grace Royal International electronically at Publisher@graceroyal-intl.com.

Atlanta, GA
Subject: Poetry

ISBN: 978-0-578-31926-1

PRINTED IN THE UNITED STATES OF AMERICA

*For my amazing daughter,
Ariona Charmain Porter
who taught me the real meaning of Love.*

*For the amazing artist of my cover
Felton J. "Bud" Galliano
Thank you for blessing me with your gift.
Artistry is an adventure behind the walls of the
eyes of a dreamer. I love your hustle.
Keep hustling.*

*For my therapist whom encouraged me to
journal, journal, journal
if it was not for their instructions I never would
have discovered this gift.
I am most grateful to
Ms. Yolanda (DeKalb Rape Crisis),
Mr. Warren Mitchell
(Journey of Self Discovery)
and Dr. Janine Howard (Abundant Mercy
Christain Church).*

*Last but not least, I dedicate this book to
Jesus Christ, My Lord And My Savior*

Love is unconditional.

In life people will use, abuse and take your love for granted...

> Leaving
> > you
> > > heartbroken.

However, because God is love, he used my amazing daughter to show me that regardless of our painful past, we still have the capacity to love.

There are some you may continue to love closely and some that you must love from afar, which is all that God requires us to do is to love.

LET MY LOVE STORY BEGIN

I am a Butterfly

I survived

My wings are now stretched wide

But, where am I going?

As far as my wings will fly!

I am a Butterfly

I survived

No longer will I settle

No longer will I faint

I survived.

One of my wings may be broken,

but

I still fly!

Colorful

Vibrant

Alive

I still fly!

Because...

I am a Butterfly.

The Birth of a Butterfly

SaSumthing!!

This phrase came to me during a conversation with my Big Sis.
SaSumthing means exactly what it says, SaSumthing!
Stop being silent with past, present and unexplained hurts.
Keeping silent is what stunts our growth
So, I ask of you after reading my Love story that you will get tuned in with the Holy spirit.
SaSumthing!
It's not OK.

Being silent is a set up for
bondage,
bitterness
and an abundance of bruises which will stunt your growth.

I challenge every reader to release and SaSumthing.

Let's Be Free

Wanting Love, wanting to give Love
so badly
left me with the aroma of
I'll take it.
So everytime I was sniffed
regardless of the situation or the circum-
stance my scent filled the room with the
fragrance of I'll Take It.
That smell
They Loved.
So I took what I thought was my best.

An Empty Cup Has

Nothing Pouring Out of It!

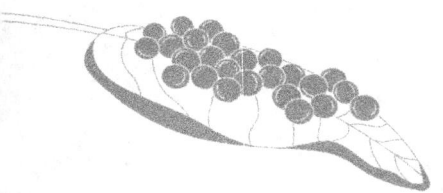

THE EGGS: FIRST STAGE

A Motherless Child

Abused, Abandoned, then Murdered
My Mom was a Motherless child
Cancer took my Mom
Now I'm a Motherless child
Cancer had no Mom
Cancer was a Motherless child
I got rules.........
Aren't children born with Mothers?
Children shouldn't live without a
Mother
Who's supposed to love the Motherless
child?
I got rules.........
Who's supposed to Love the Motherless child?

What is a Motherless child to do?

A Father's Love

A chipped Mug
Daughter, A tea cup without a handle
A heart but no beat
Daughter, screaming with no sound
What is A Father's Love?
Broken, Bitter and Bruised
How does he love A Daughter?
Instructions not provided
No School Zone
Daughter, seeds planted that wasn't
expected to grow
What is A Father's Love?
I should have killed you
The enemy
Daughter, in the midst of War
Shoots fired
Daughter, do I shoot back?
Daughter, or should I die not ever
knowing
The question still stands

What is A Father's Love ???

Sister's Love

A Sister's Love
My sister, my friend, my Mother's
Love
A Sister's Love
Is wider than the ocean and the sea
A Sister's Love
Sticks like glue
A Sister's Love
Is sweeter than sugar
A Sister's Love
Was ordained by God
A Sister's Love
Unconditional
A Sister's Love
Was God sent
Does everybody have Sisters like me?
A Sister's Love

I Thank You All.....

The Caterpillar: Second Stage

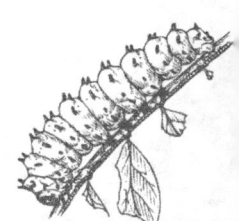

Bullet Proof

Shot in the heart but it's still beating
Shown no signs of blood
Shoved in the closet
Locked doors.....
Scared? No
Confused? Yes
Surprised?........ Shrug Shoulders....
Sweet tooth for Setbacks
Stuck on Stupid
Signals un-read
Sirens going off
Silent Sreams
Seasoned with No flavor
Shot with a 45.
Still breathing
Shamed into Silence
Steel is what my heart is made of...
What's yours made of?

Thirteen and Thirsty

I missed the signs.......
Touched but No feelings
Torn without Understanding
Thirteen now Twenty-Three
Ten years
Where did time go?
Trapped in a Horror,
no where to Turn
Tipsy off abuse.......Strung out
Tunnel vision,
I can't see but,
I know I'm wounded
Tangled in Love, Lust, Lies
or is it Truth?

I didn't know, did you?

LOVE never Loved Me
Love Lied
Love was Hurtful
Love was One Sided
Love was Faithful...Not!
Love broke My Heart
Love didn't Change
Love ruined My Friendship
Love was Fake
Love Walked out
Love Put me out
Love Raped us
Love Just let go
Love loved Someone Else
Love never Apologized......................
I vote to Never Love AGAIN!

Firecrackers In My Mind

Snap, Crackle, Pop
Will it ever Stop?
Firecrackers in my Mind
Boom, Fizzle, Bam
What's going on?
Damn
Who is responsible for this?
Firecrackers in my Mind
Sparkles, Flash, Shine
What's going on in my mind
Will the pain ever stop?
Who knows?
My mind might just pop.
Why do people stand and watch
When I'm hurting inside?
Why do I have Firecrackers in my
Mind?

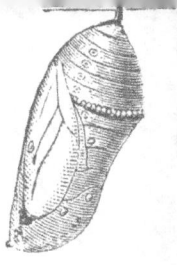

The Chrysalis:
Third Stage

Love Never Loved Me

A street light with no bulb
Love.
It Never Loved Me
A pencil with no lead
Love Didn't Love Me
A car with no engine
Love Never Loved Me
A flute with no sound
Love Never Loved Me
Love was ?

My Darling Daniel

You disrespected me
You hurt me
And left me angry
Drugs was never an option
now it's a thought
Males were created to protect
Instead you left me in pain
As if you had no home training
Where did this come from?
What's in your background?
Now I'm lost
Stuck in a state of confusion
Left to regret it all
I feel all alone and lonely
Why was liars created?
I never heard an apology
I wonder will I have this pain forever?
Praise God I didn't keep quiet
Now I'm unstoppable…………………

#sasumthing

My Grace

Is it Grace?
Or
Is it Mercy?
Her name
Ariona Charmain
Grace
I didn't deserve her
Mercy
But he gave her to me
Precious she is
Unique she is
Wonderful Yes!
My sparkle
What a gift...
Thank you Lord for having Mercy
on me and giving me Grace......

One Broken Heart To Another

How do you love when your heart is
Broken?
A broken heart can't mend another
Broken pieces seem to find another
Broke
Broken
Broken-Hearted
Beat down
Bruised
Bipolar
No Prescription
No Diagnosis
Yet I still don't know how do I mend a
Broken heart
How is it that the Broken seeks to heal
the Broke
Is it a scent that I leave?
Or is it a sign on my back?
Everyone needs to be loved or do they?
My chest is a glass box that displayed
the cracks in my heart
One Broken Heart to another.

Love 'n Basketball

Love didn't play fair
Love would give me the
Ball, yet steal it back again.
Love would pat me on the
Butt, yet just to get close again.
Basketball had a heart
But, Love didn't
Love, what is it? A Game?
Yes, I think so.
Do you just play the game
Knowing you're going to Lose?
Where was the Coach?
One player is more advanced
than the others.
Should he be disqualified?
I think so. ....
I'm out of the game
I promise never
To Play Basketball AGAIN!

The Love of the Game

B-ball
Play ball
Dribble
Whistle blowing
Free throws
Three pointers
Basketball
Net
Coach
Dollar bills
Screaming
Shouting
Cheering
I had all that was required
But I still lost the game...

My Glass is Always Half Full

My Glass may never run over
But am I Loved?

My Glass is full
but never full enough to run over
Am I Loved?
My Glass has a few cracks, scraps &
chips
but never been broken
Am I Loved?
My Glass once leaked
but now it's sealed
Am I Loved?

Wow!
I have found the answer
Even though God has refurbished
my Glass it may never run over.....
But I am Loved?
I'm sick and no one's here
But am I Loved?

I may never know..........................
Was it worth it?
Truth is I'll never know........
Un-invested Heart
Just Curiosity.............
Goodbye My Love

Poisoned Over the Phone

Every time the Phone rings
It's like drinking Poison
Poison over the Phone not in a
Bottle
Why did Love bring me here?
Am I not Loved at all?
The phone rings, I Drink
Why would you Poison me?
My heart beats for You
My reward is drink
You Fool
The phone rings, I Drink
I'm slowly Dying
My heart still Beats
Things will never Change
How did I get here?
Oh! I Forgot.
"Love"
My heart beats Slower
The phone rings, I Drink
Every time we talk I get Weaker

Why am I not getting stronger?
The phone rings, I Drink
I'm weak, I won't make it
I'm dying
Do you even Know
The phone rings, I can barely
Swallow
But I Drink
I'm Down, Damn.......

....
I've flat lined
Wow!
My heart Stopped
Did I commit Suicide?
Will God forgive Me for taking
Poison?
Did you Kill me?
Will God forgive You for Poisoning
Me?
You said if I Die, you'll just move
on...

      Why was I poisoned?

How do you let go?

How do you let go of a broken
string?
How do you let go
when your heart still beats with
no oxygen?
How is the plant still living with
No water?
How do you let go?
Questions, No Answers
How do you let go
when it's nothing there?
How is it that your hand is being
held but no one's there
Why is it that my heart is broken
but still in one piece?
Just how do you let go?

Whose Going to Love Me?

Whose Going to Love Me?
Me
Whose going to Pray for me?
Me
Whose going to Encourage me?
Me
Whose going to Motivate me?
Me
Whose going to Believe in me?
Me
Whose going to say nice things to me?
Me
Whose going to Celebrate me?
Me
Whose going to have my Back?
Jesus

A Daddy's Love

He loves his girls
One, Two, Three
Girls, Girls, Girls
This is his World
God praises a Man that Loves his
Girls
Girls, Girls, Girls
This is his World
Not third, not second
First
Girls, Girls, Girls
This is his World
I fell in love with a Man that Loves
his girls

True Love

True love. What is it?
I can't answer, I never had it.
Should it have first been with my
Dad?
I can't answer
I never experienced it.
Love me, Leave me and cheat on me
is that it?
I can't answer I never felt it...
How is it that I yearn to be loved?
I can't answer
I never had it....

In remembrance...
I do remember once being Loved
unfortunately that Love died with
him.......
May he Rest in Peace with True Love
GoodBye True Love
May we meet again

INTOXICATED LOVE

Sober, Hey Heat
Intoxicated, I Love You
Sober, How's your day?
Intoxicated, I'm Happy
Sober, Have A Blessed day
Intoxicated, Missing you
Sober, What you doing today
Intoxicated, You're my woman
Sober, Be patient
Intoxicated, I see us having a future
Sober, Things are going to change
Intoxicated, I'm going to Marry you
Sober, Confused
Is there any truth in Intoxicated Love?

The Beautiful Butterfly:
FINAL Stage

Live Your Truth

What's your truth?
Hhhmmmmm
My Truth....
I'm a woman?
True
I have baggage?
True
I'm a work in progress?
True
I've committed adultery?
True
I couldn't see my way through?
True
I've settled?
True

I didn't know my worth?
True
I just wanted to be loved?
True
I wanted to be needed?
True
I wanted to take care of someone?
True
I wanted a family?
True
I wanted to belong to somebody?
True
What do I need?
Jesus
What do I have?
Jesus

Dre Day

Wow! WOW!
What a mighty God we serve
MYTIGOD
Love is loving me
Love promised
Love did it
I walked out
Love came and got me
I thought not
Love showed me different
I gave up
Love didn't
I cried
Love wiped my tears
I smile
And
Love said I Will You
I said YES
I Do?
2017

Will You?

Will you Marry Me?
Yes
My Love is meant to steal, kill and destroy!
Will You?
I'm Numb.. no emotions and no feelings.
Will You?
Familiar territory!
Will You?
Why did I say yes?
Am I Crazy or Lost?
Will You?
I Can't...

How do you Love a Broken Hearted Man?

How do we communicate when he's so sensitive
A boy stuck in a man's dream
A father that doesn't know how to embrace Love
Broken, bruised and confused
How do you Love the broken-hearted
So accustomed to pretending he knows no truth
Lost, abandoned and self-destructing
Flavor his life with false pretenses
No one knows, but I can see
How do you Love the broken-hearted
A cause way to common
in our community
Someone please help heal the broken-hearted
Or can they be healed?
Who can heal the broken-hearted?
To be continued...........

I Am?

I am Black
I am Loyal
I am Beautiful
I am Bothered
I am Royal
I am Bold
I am Victorious
I am Tired
I am Blessed
I am Grateful
I am Wise
I am Numb
I am the Mother of the Ungratefuls....

A B-Momma's Love

I'm a Bonus Momma
Not a Step-Momma
Steps you walk on
Bonus you walk with
He said your steps are ordered
Multiply not Divide
He said Add not Subtract
God said Go
and fill their tanks
tune their engines
My babies are driving
No Licence or Insurance
If they are arrested then I shall be
charged
Orange is not the new Black
No shades of Grey
I make my Vow to my sweet girls
The 3 Blind mice
To Love, Honor, Respect and
Cherish
All the days of our lives

Tune up complete, tires rotated
Engine running
we headed to the DMV on Love
Lane
Will they pass the test?
Yes, they will
Thank You Jesus!
His word stands True
"I shall give You, Your heart
desires"
The 3 Blind mice..........

A FOOL and Her Money will soon
depart
I love Purses
I love shoes
I love clothes
Well Hell
I love to shop
A fool I was who departed from her
money
Sad, Mad, Glad
No
Grateful for God's Grace

Love, What Is It?

What is Love??????
Love is Valerie Driskell
If you've ever crossed her path,
you experienced Love
If you called her
You've heard Love
If she washed your hair
you've felt Love
If she came to see you
You saw Love
If you hug her
You've smelled Love
If you've made a purchase from her
You've wore Love
God blessed us all with Val's
Love.........
Thank you.........

Search Your Soul

I searched
I search, I search, I search
I search my soul and it's full
I search my heart and it's pure
I search my mind and it's strong
I search my soul and it's genuine
I search, I search, I search

Women are Jewels

Some Diamonds in the rough
Some Shinning Rubies at birth
Some Upcoming Pearls
Some Gold and Silver needing to
be polished

But why are some sitting by the
Trash?
Why are some Thrown away?
Why are some Abused?
Why are some Abandoned?
Wow!! Where do we Go?

Women, we must remember
-Our life is not ours-
It belongs to the Lord
Therefore, we were never given permission
To allow ourselves to be Misused, Overlooked, Abused, or Abandoned

"A man who finds a wife finds what is good and receives Favor from the Lord"
Where do we Go?
Go and be a Victorious Woman

Love me, Love me not
What is Love?
Lies, truth, hurt and pain
How do you Love when you don't
Love yourself
Loving requires self-love
Don't Love me Love yourself!

Why Do I Love Thee?

I was blessed this morning to understand why our relationship struggles so......reason is, you being a man & me being a woman we think on different sides of the table.

Over the past 7 days I've been puzzled to the point of confusion (not of God) to be provided with the understanding that what you first sought me for was less than ((-), minus, low, below, etc.) not Queen status.

That's why we bumped heads because you can't see me, provide for me, take care of me, love me for who I am. A Queen.

*To be given wisdom is a Blessing and a curse for those who don't possess it.

Who chooses who?
When you choose to love someone whose been broken, battered and abused you must know that any imperfection that you see should never be the focal point of your conversation.

Choosing to love someone that never believed that true love would find them will first a foremost require patience.

And, don't make your love a liar too.

A Judge's Love

Am I the right candidate
Is my work not good enough
No. my heart is pure
But that's not enough
Why am I being Judged
because I Love my work?
My work is my Art
I'm quitting

My emotions dissect
A chemistry project
He says there's No other like you
You must stay
Push through
Keep cutting

A gross smell that I'll never forget
Let it soak for a while
I try again.
Yuck
I'm done

Keep trying
I try again
Read this book
I read
I'm kicked out
Why?
I failed
The Jury's Verdict
Nope I passed
Wow! We meet again
Our work shall continue

To Be Continued.........
?????????????
READ THE DAILY REPORT

Love 101

Love should be taught in preschool because Love is something we all take for granted ooh so regularly. Would the world be better if we just hated? Because Loving others to be rejected doesn't seem fair. Love can't be given if it's first not truly experienced or taught. So sad how we mis-love someone searching for a dead end. So sad how we mis-love trying to prove a point that will never be understood. So sad how we mis-love because we don't want to say I'm sorry. So sad how we mis-love seeking for what you already have. So sad how we mis-love by not closing doors that should've never been open. So sad how we mis-love by hanging on to the past that you keep in your future.
Don't let love miss you.
It may never return.

Born

Born
Died at 5
Now living what I've dreamed
Flying
Soaring to the highest heights.
Dead but yet alive
Died at 5
I've birth a dream that is birthing
one too.
I was born to die
But yet I'm alive, cause I died at
5.

Love Found My Love and Gave Birth!

Grace - blessed me with my Love.
I didn't deserve it but God said,
"You're purposed." Who me? Wow!
Thank you. I'm grateful.

I've been turned and flipped, but
why? Who me? Again God said,
"Yes, you my child."

Grace, Grace - blessed me with my
Love's Love, she deserves it, God says
"Yes, she's designed by my purpose."
Me? Wow!

Thank you, Thank you, so, so grateful.
I've been turned, flipped and crowned,
but why? Who me? Me? Again!
God says, "Yes, you my child!"

Grace, Grace and more grace -
blessed me with my Love's Love and
Heaven sent.

Yes, she deserves it.
She's designed by my purpose.
I thank you Lord for your Grace
which I don't deserve and your
Mercy which I didn't earn.
I will forever be Grateful!!!!!!

I Love You, Yia Yia

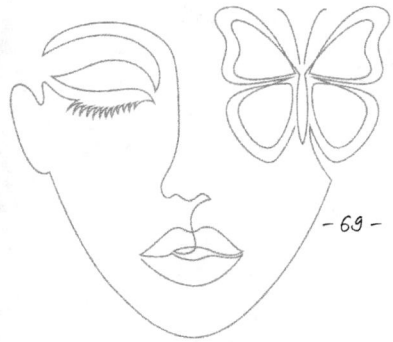

I Stepped Outside My Box

I stepped outside of my Box when
I stepped out my Mother's womb...
I stepped outside my Box when I
lived after my Mother died....
Confused, dizzy and numb
I stepped outside of my Box when
my Father misunderstood me.....
Abandoned, Loveless and Lost
I stepped outside of my Box when
I graduated and was told I would
never be shit....
Low, Lifeless and Lonely
I stepped outside my Box when I
was asked "Will you be my Wife"
three times and still believed in
Love.....
Broken, Battered, and Abused
I stepped outside my Box when I
was told "Die Bitch...."
Stomped, drugged and punched

I stepped outside my Box when I
raised my baby girl to be a woman
of Grace
Virtuous, refined and beautiful
I stepped out of my Box when I
earned three degrees
AA, BA and MBA
I stepped outside my Box when I
was let go from my dream job...
Blessing...My steps were ordered
I stepped outside my Box when I
choose to give Love versus hate
So just push through the four
walls; they were made of paper...
I dare you...
Step outside your Box and see
what happens
I was born with no intention of
surviving

But, I'm ALIVE!

Longlivezay4l

Born first
Died first
The last shall be the first and the first shall be last
What place do I hold?
Mom loves me, Mom loves me not
Who am I ?
Was I not worthy or was I chosen for a wake up call?
Did they get it or was I a lost cause?
Was I protected or was I failed?
Who should now face these charges?
I know not me.
God,
Please Forgive Me for my sins because you forgave them for failing me........
Silence is the lamb...........

Longlivezay4l

My Children
Why do they die before their time?

When a child dies before their time it's like playing a tape that you fast forward, and ripping the tape out where it will never play again.
I will often wonder if we let that tape play what sounds would we have heard?
Could it have been Jazz a sweet sound with a nice melody with no words?
Or could it have been Reggae a hard beat but a smooth vibe?
How about Gospel a spiritual message behind a nice beat?
Ooh Wayment! Rap a nasty beat with a true message?
Sad to say we will never know what tune Eli wanted to play.

Jamilriya Lester

You are my kind of Beautiful!
you are Black
you are Bold
you are Bright
you are Brave
you are Big-hearted
you are Benevolent
you are Blithe
you are Beloved
you are a Boss
Continue to be great...

-Love

THE LOVE

The Love that a Motherless Mom
can give.
Even though there's a hole in my
heart, my heart is full of love to
give.
God felt my pain and blessed me
all the same
Now I'm a Mother who's gained.
Now I'm a Mother with a name
Yia Yia is my name.

Butterflies Fly

You're a Beautiful Butterfly
Butterflies fly and sprinkle aaahhh's
You're a Butterfly not a Bird!
Butterflies fly
Birds carry mess
Butterflies will fly by you and give
you a kiss
Birds will peck you in the head
A Butterfly will fly pass shit
A Bird will carry shit
A broken wing Butterfly can still fly
A broken wing Bird is crippled
A Butterfly will leave you in awe
A Bird will make you wonder what's
their next move
Butterflies don't carry loads
A Bird will always try
Fly my Beautiful Butterfly you're not
a Bird!
Wing Broken Still Beautiful Still
Flying High!!
Now you can say that you have
seen a Butterfly with a Broken
Wing.............

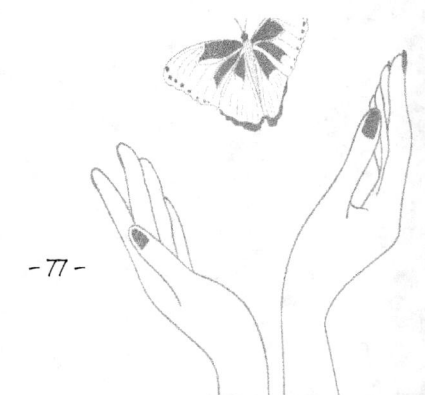

Death is so Disrespectful!

How do you handle life when death
has disrespected you?
You are blind-sided
when it makes itself present
Disrespectful!
short notice or no notice at all.
Disrespectful!
How do you press forward
when you have no push to go on?
Disrespectful!
Why is death so disrespectful?
The Answer is Love!
Love when you don't want to
Love when they're mad at you
Love when they've made a mistake
Love when your patience runs out
Love when you just don't know
what else to do
Love conquers All
And Love is Life!
Let's not be so disrespectful......
LOVE while you have breath.

Am I Grieving Or Is This Mental Health?

My body is numb and my tear
bucket is full.
H. Help me God!
Am I a lost cause
or should I be medicated?
My mind is all over the place
and I am confused.
H. Hold me Lord!
Am I going to make it or will I
perish?
My soul cries out and I must pray.
B. But God I am Free!
I Miss My Daddy!
Open the door God it's **H. H. B.**
Heaven gained a new Angel !
I Love You Daddy........

I AM A BUTTERFLY
I CAN FLY
WING MAY BE BROKEN
BUT JUST WATCH ME FLY
WHEN YOU SEE ME GO BY
JUST SAY OOOH AAAAH
AND WATCH ME GO BY

-SIGNED
   A BROKEN WING
   BUTTERFLY!

YOUR JOURNAL

MORE BY SUMMER HEAT

Butterflies & Lemonade

ABOUT THE AUTHOR

Summer Heat is the founder & CEO of
AnowA Foundation, Inc. --
A nonprofit organization dedicated to providing support & rehabilitation for sexually abused adolescents along with adult survivors of child sexual abuse & domestic violence.

Summer Heat is the proud grandmother of two boys. She currently resides in the Atlanta Metropolitan Area.

Visit www.sasumthing.org to learn more.

#sasumthing
It's Not OK.

www.ingramcontent.com/pod-product-compliance
Lightning Source LLC
Chambersburg PA
CBHW072015290426
44109CB00018B/2247